ENCHANTING FAIRY-TALE
CRAFTS

by Marne Ventura

4D™

An Augmented Reading
Crafting
Experience

CAPSTONE PRESS
a capstone imprint

Dabble Lab Books are published by Capstone Press,
1710 Roe Crest Drive
North Mankato, Minnesota 56003

www.mycapstone.com

Library of Congress Cataloging-in-Publication Data
Cataloging-in-Publication Data is available on the Library of Congress website.
ISBN 978-1-5435-0689-1 (library binding)
ISBN 978-1-5435-0693-8 (eBook PDF)

Editorial Credits
Mari Bolte, editor; Lori Bye, designer; Morgan Walters, media researcher;
Kathy McColley, production specialist

Photo Credits: All photographs by Capstone Studio/Karon Dubke except:
Shutterstock: CkyBe, design element throughout, Neti.OneLove, design element
throughout

Printed and bound in the USA.
010760S18

TABLE OF CONTENTS

Once upon a time . . .

. . . fairies and ogres lived in enchanted forests. Humans in nearby castles were caught in the struggle between good and evil. Fortunately, most lived happily ever after.

If you love the world of fairy tales, you can use this book to make some of your favorite characters and scenes. Customize each project to match the kingdoms and castles that live in your imagination.

Are you ready to enter the land of far, far, away? Just read over the directions, gather up your supplies, and start adding your own magic touches!

Download the Capstone 4D app!

- Ask an adult to search in the Apple App Store or Google Play for "Capstone 4D".
- Click Install (Android) or Get, then Install (Apple).
- Open the app.
- Scan any of the following spreads with this icon:

When you scan a spread, you'll find fun extra stuff to go with this book! You can also find these things on the web at *www.capstone4D.com* using the password: ncc.fairytales

THUMBELINA'S
GARDEN

Thumbelina grew inside a tulip bud. She played beneath the flowers and slept in a walnut shell. Recreate Thumbelina's Garden in your own magical terrarium.

What You'll Need:

small pebbles
glass jar
shredded book
    pages or
    newspaper
moss
seed pods and bark
artificial flowers

modeling clay
scissors
wooden toothpicks
jumbo craft stick
marker
hot glue and hot
    glue gun

1.

2.

Steps:

1. Pour a layer of pebbles into the jar.

2. Add a layer of shredded book pages.

3. Layer moss over the pebbles.

4. Add pods and bark.

4.

5. Push the stems of the artificial flowers through the moss and into the layer of pebbles.

6. To make a toadstool, roll a piece of modeling clay into a ball. Flatten the bottom to shape into a mushroom cap.

7. Cut off and discard one end of a toothpick. Push the trimmed end into the clay. Cover part of the toothpick with modeling clay before pushing it into the moss.

8. Make a garden sign by cutting the craft stick into smaller pieces. Write a message onto the stick.

9. Cut the trimmed end lengthwise to make a post for the sign. Hot glue the sign to the post.

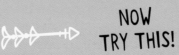

NOW TRY THIS!

Add miniature figures to your terrarium. Use a half walnut shell and green leaf for Thumbelina's bed and blanket.

ENCHANTED FOREST

Hansel and Gretel are lost and alone in the dark forest. Help them find their way by lighting up the sky.

What You'll Need:

paint and paintbrush
sturdy box with fold
    out lid
towel
hammer and nail
battery operated
    LED lights
lids 3 to 9 inches (7.6
    to 23 centimeters)
    wide

book pages
pencil
scissors
clear tape
white glue
small pebbles

Steps:

1. Paint the outside of the box. Let it dry completely.

2. Paint or draw decorations on the inside of the box. A spooky forest, a haunted house, or a cozy cottage are only a few ideas.

3. Lay the box open-side-up on a folded towel. Have an adult punch holes with the hammer and nail in the bottom of the box.

4. Turn the box over. Push the lights through the holes.

5. Set the lids onto the book pages. Trace and cut out one circle of each size.

6. Fold each circle in half, and then cut along the fold to make six half-circles.

7. Curve each half-circle into tree shapes, and tape the edges together.

8. Cut a piece of decorative paper to fit the bottom of the box. Glue in place. Then cut a path out of the book pages, and glue that to the paper.

9. Glue rocks onto the path. Make sure some of the paper shows around the edges. Place the trees along the pathway, and glue in place.

10. Decorate your enchanted forest with small branches, rocks, or colorful pom-poms.

NOW TRY THIS!

Use markers to draw a gingerbread house on cardstock. Glue to the inside back of the box. You could also add a real gingerbread house!

BOOK LOVER'S PLACE
KEEPER

Rescue an old hardbound book on its last legs.
Use the spine to make a pretty bookmark.
Save the rest of the book for other projects.

What You'll Need:

craft knife
hardcover book
scissors
spray adhesive
hole punch

embroidery
thread
ruler
pencil

1.

Steps:

1. Ask an adult to cut the spine from book.

2. Cut a page from the book. Set the front and back cover and other pages aside for other crafts.

3. Spray the back of the spine with adhesive. Press the book page onto the glue. Let it dry completely. Then trim the page so it's the same size as the spine.

4. Punch a hole at the top of the spine.

5. Cut six 1 yard (0.9 meter) pieces of embroidery thread. Line up the threads, and fold them in half.

6. Slip the thread onto the pencil. Hold the loose ends of the thread with your other hand. Stretch the thread taut.

7. Wind the pencil around and around so that the thread twists upon itself. Make 40 twists.

8. Remove the pencil. Keep the thread taut as you slip it through the hole in the bookmark.

9. Ask a friend to hold the bookmark. Bring the ends of the cord together. The sides will twist around each other.

10. Tie the ends of the thread together.

2.

3.

6.

8.

NOW TRY THIS!

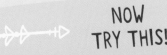

Use felt as backing for the spine. Use a sewing machine to make stitches around the edges. Add a 1/2 inch (1.3 cm) eyelet instead of punching a hole.

WAKE UP, SLEEPING
BEAUTY

The wicked fairy put a spell on the princess, and everyone
in the castle fell into a deep sleep. Build your own
castle and catapult to fight your way in! Find some friends
and see who can hurl the most ammo over the battlements
and into the castle courtyard.

What You'll Need:

scissors
cardboard box
4 cardboard tubes
hot glue and hot
   glue gun
pencil
craft knife
nail

two 12-inch
  (30.5-cm)-long
   pieces of string
colored cardstock
old book pages
toothpicks
9 craft sticks
rubber bands
plastic bottle cap

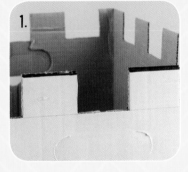

Steps:

1. Cut the lid flaps from the box. Have an adult help
    you cut out squares along the top of the box. These
    are the battlements.

2. Draw windows and a drawbridge on the front of the
    box. Ask an adult to cut them out with a craft knife.

3. Use the nail to poke a hole on the left side of the
    drawbridge. Poke another hole in the castle, near
    the top of the door hole.

4. Tie a knot at one end of the string. Push the other
    end of the string through the drawbridge hole.
    Then run the string through the hole in the castle.
    Tie a knot in the string, and trim the ends.

5. Repeat steps 3 and 4 on the right side of
    the drawbridge.

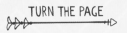
TURN THE PAGE

6. Make flags for your castle using the construction paper and old book pages. Use toothpicks as flag poles. Glue them to the battlements.

7. To make the catapult, stack 7 craft sticks on top of each other. Secure both ends with a rubber band.

8. Stack two craft sticks on top of each other. Attach them at one end with a rubber band. Slide the bottom stick between the first and second sticks in the stack of 7. This stick should be facing the opposite direction. The top stick should sit on top of the stack of 7.

9. Hot glue the bottle cap to the free end of the upper stick. Let dry completely.

10. Place the castle on a table or the floor. Place the catapult a few feet in front of the castle.

11. Cut the book pages into small pieces. Then roll each piece into tight balls.

12. Set a paper cannonball in the bottle cap. Hold the base of the catapult with one finger, push down the edge of the bottle cap, and release.

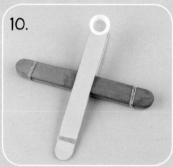

13. The player who lands the most cannonballs inside the castle wins!

NOW TRY THIS!

Shoot cotton balls, pom-poms, or mini marshmallows instead of paper.

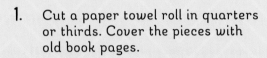

NOW TRY THIS!

Is your castle in the middle of an enchanted forest? It can be! Add a tree or two. For an extra spooky forest, slip battery-operated tea lights into the paper towel tubes. Flip them on, and turn off the lights!

1. Cut a paper towel roll in quarters or thirds. Cover the pieces with old book pages.

2. Measure the width of the tube. Mark two lines on each cloud shape to match that width. Then cut the slits about 1 inch (2.5 cm). Slide each cloud shape onto the top of a roll to make a tree.

3. Make as many or as few trees as you want! Use different shades of green to give your forest a more realistic look.

FIND A
FLOWER

An enchanted rose kept the Beast a prisoner in his castle. Make yourself a flower that lasts forever—and doesn't come with a spell attached.

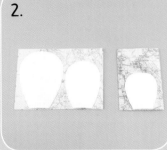

What You'll Need:

cardstock
12-by-16 inch (30.5-by-40.6 cm)
    pages from an old atlas
scissors
glue

Steps:

1. Cut out a large petal shape with a flat bottom out of the cardstock. Repeat, but make a slightly smaller petal. Then make a third, even smaller, petal.

2. Use the large cardstock petal as a template to trace and cut out a petal from the atlas pages. Repeat until you have six large petals.

3. Repeat step 2 with the medium- and small-sized templates. Make six of each size petal. Curl the wide ends of the petals in slightly.

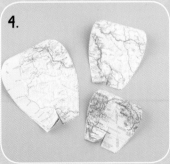

4. Cut a 2-inch (5-cm) slit at the bottom of each petal.

5. Slightly overlap the paper on either side of the slit. Glue into place.

TURN THE PAGE

6. Attach two petals to each other with glue. They should overlap slightly.

7. Keep adding petals until they're all attached. You should have a bowl shape. Let the glue dry completely.

8. Repeat steps 1–5 with the medium-sized petals.

9. Repeat steps 1–5 with the smallest petals.

10. Flip the large bowl over. Glue a small piece of cardstock to the bottom. This will make it easier to hang your flowers later.

11. Glue the small bowl into the medium bowl. Then glue the medium bowl into the large bowl.

12. To make the center of the flower, stack three sheets of atlas paper on top of each other. Cut the sheets in half the long way. Discard one half.

13. Fold the paper in half the long way.

14. Make cuts down the folded edge. Leave about ½ inch (1.3 cm) of uncut paper along the other edge.

15. Separate the papers and glue the short ends together so you have one long piece.

16. Roll the papers into a tight tube. The uncut edge is the base. Fluff the fringe as you roll.

17. Glue the end of the tube shut. Then glue the flat end into the center of the flower.

NOW TRY THIS!

Use mounting tape to hang your flowers on a wall. Then add stems and leaves with green washi tape. Place vases next to the wall to make it look like the flowers are arranged.

SPELLS AND POTIONS
BOOK

Cinderella's fairy godmother turned a pumpkin into a coach. What would you do with magic? Bind your own spell book and find out for yourself!

What You'll Need:

scissors
magazine
old hardback book
decoupage glue and paintbrush
5 sheets of 8.5-by-11 inch
    (21.6-by-28-cm) copy paper
clear tape

Steps:

1. Cut letters from a magazine to write "SPELLS & POTIONS." Cut out other designs to decorate the cover.

2. Paint a thin layer of decoupage glue onto the cover. Arrange your letters and designs how you want them. Then paint a thin layer of decoupage glue over the top. Let dry completely.

3. Stack the copy paper. Fold in half.

4. Open the first page of the folded book. Center a strip of clear tape along the fold. Press down firmly.

5. Turn to the next page and repeat until all of the pages are taped.

6. Set the pages inside the book cover. Trim to fit, if necessary.

NOW TRY THIS!

Instead of cutting out letters, write the title by squirting white glue on the cover. Sprinkle with gold glitter.

MAGIC
WAND

Now that you have a spell book, you
need a magic wand. Abracadabra!

What You'll Need:

white glue
8.5-by-11-inch
    (21.6-by-28-cm)
    piece of cardstock
12-inch (30.5-cm)-long
    piece of 3/8-inch
    (1-cm) wooden
    dowel

scissors
large clear gem
smaller gem
hot glue gun
metallic or glitter paint

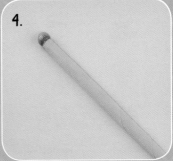

Steps:

1. Drizzle white glue over one side of the cardstock.

2. Starting at one corner, roll the cardstock around the dowel at a diagonal. Smooth out any wrinkles. Let the glue dry completely.

3. Remove the dowel.

4. Fill one end of the tube with hot glue. Stick the large gem on the end.

5. Fill the other end of the tube with hot glue. Stick the small gem on the end.

6. Use the hot glue gun to make a design on the wand.

7. Paint the wand.

8. Add accents with a second paint color.

24

PIXIE DUST
NECKLACE

Where do fairy godmothers and pixies store their magic dust? This tiny bottle on a ribbon is the perfect solution. Practical, and pretty too!

What You'll Need:

1/2 inch (1.3 cm) eye screw
tiny bottle with cork
glitter in various colors
hole punch
old book pages
clear nail polish
1/4-inch (.6-cm)-wide ribbon
1/4-inch-wide ribbon end cap and clasp
crimping tool

Steps:

1. Screw the eye into the center of the bottle's cork.

2. Line your work surface with newspaper. With an adult's help, pour glitter into the bottle. Fill the bottle about two-thirds of the way full.

3. Use a hole punch to make shapes out of the old book pages.

4. Carefully pour the shapes into the bottle.

5. Paint a thin layer of clear nail polish around the cork. Then firmly press the cork onto the bottle.

6. Measure and cut the ribbon to fit around your neck.

7. Glue and crimp the end cap to one ribbon end.

8. Thread the other end of the ribbon through the bottle's eye screw.

9. Glue and crimp the clasp to the other end of the ribbon.

KEEP OUT CASE

Magic bags are often seen in fairy tales, myths, and legends. Make your own, and keep curious folk away with a poisonous apple on the outside.

What You'll Need:

measuring tape
light green felt
scissors
pins
red, white,
  green, brown,
  and black felt

thread
sewing machine
fabric glue
fabric marker

Steps:

1. Measure a piece of light green felt that's twice as long as the e-reader, plus 3 inches (7.6 cm). It should be 5 inches (12.7 cm) wider than the e-reader.

2. Fold the short sides of the felt in 1.5 inches (3.8 cm). Pin the folds in place.

3. Sew around the felt, about ½ inch (1.3 cm) from the edge.

4. Fold the felt rectangle in half with the hems facing inward. Pin along the long sides. Put your e-reader inside and move the pins to show where to sew the sides.

5. Remove the e-reader and sew the sides.

6. Trim the excess felt from the sewn sides.

7. Cut a red apple from felt. Cut a smaller apple from white felt. Cut a brown stem and a green leaf.

8. Hot glue the apple, stem, and leaf to the front of the e-reader case. Add seeds with a fabric marker.

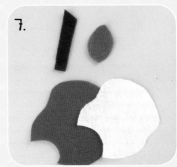

NOW TRY THIS!

Instead of an apple, sew a pocket onto the front of your case for your library card.

DELICIOUS DRAGON
EGGS

Hatch your own dragon (or just hide some delicious treats inside) these edible eggs. There will be a surprise every time!

What You'll Need:

3 tablespoons
    (45 mililters) butter
10 ounce (283 gram) bag
    of marshmallows
1 teaspoon (5 mL) vanilla
    extract
6 cups (1.5 liters) puffed
    rice cereal
food coloring (optional)

cooking spray
large spoon
large plastic egg
candy
candy melts in
    one color
candy-coated chocolate
    in the same color

Steps:

1. Ask an adult to melt butter over low heat.

2. Add marshmallows. Stir until melted. Remove from heat.

3. Stir in vanilla and food coloring, if desired. Add the cereal and mix until everything is well coated.

4. Open the plastic egg, and add a 1-inch (1.5-cm) layer of cereal all around.

5. Pour in your surprise candy.

6. Seal the plastic egg. Set aside for at least 20 minutes before unmolding.

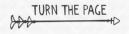
TURN THE PAGE

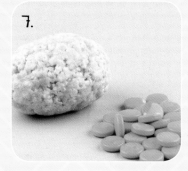

7.

7. Have an adult follow the melting instructions on the package of candy melts.

8. Use the back of a spoon to dab some candy melt onto your egg. Press a candy-coated chocolate into the candy melt.

9. Keep dabbing and adding candy pieces until the entire egg is covered. Stagger the candy so they overlap slightly.

8.

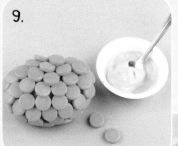

9.

NOW TRY THIS!

Use edible spray paint or glitter to coat the outside of the egg.

Edible glitter, gold leaf, luster dust, disco dust, jewel dust, and petal dust are all safe ways you can add some sparkle.

CHECK OUT ALL OF THE NEXT CHAPTER CRAFTS SERIES!

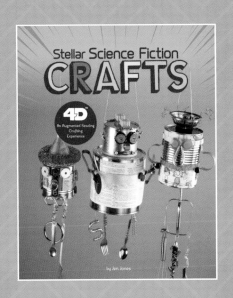

ONLY FROM CAPSTONE!

READ MORE

Bertolazzi, Alberto. *Beauty and the Beast Origami.* New York: Dover Publications, 2017.

Harbo, Christopher L. *Sock Puppet Theater Presents Little Red Riding Hood: A Make & Play Production.* North Mankato, Minn.: Capstone Press, 2018.

MAKERSPACE TIPS

Download tips and tricks for using this book and others in a library makerspace.

Visit www.capstonepub.com/dabblelabresources

INTERNET SITES

Use FactHound to find Internet sites related to this book.

Visit www.facthound.com

Just type in 9781543506891 and go.